Step by Step: Write, Self-Publish, and Market Your Book

A handbook to help make your writing dreams come true by Bett Correa

Step by Step: Write, Self-publish, and Market Your Book

Product of the United States of America

Publisher's Cataloging-in-Publication data
Correa, Bett.
A title of the book : Step by Step: Write, Self-Publish, and Market Your Book.
ISBN-13: 978-1497550933

1. The main category of the book — Reference / Writing Skills

First Edition

Editing: Russil Tamsen

Bett Correa

Dedication and Thanks

This book is for all the people who have something amazing to write about. Please share your precious book with us! We want to read it.

Thank you to my wonderful editor Russil Tamsen who is a true partner in my creative writing endeavors. Thank you to all of my friends who are such big supporters of my work.

Contents

Chapter 1 Introduction

Do you dream of writing and publishing your own book? Stop dreaming and start doing! It's not anywhere as hard as you think. It took me thirteen months from the time I started writing my book to the day I published it on Amazon.com.

Do you want to document some area of research, or need to establish yourself as an expert in some area? Speakers who have published a book get twice as much per diem as non-writers. Being a published author can help you get promoted or land a new job. You might have many reasons to write and publish. This book is written for you.

This small handbook is a step-by-step with pictures on how to write, publish, and market your book. I've learned many things the hard way, so you don't need to!

Self-publishing is a great way to get your work out into the world, but it isn't for everyone. How do you know you want to self-publish? I've included some ideas around options if you were thinking of going through a traditional publisher in the references section.

How to read this book:

I've put the chapter on marketing your book first. It will lay out some critical steps for the success of your venture. Also, setting out with the end in mind can help you stay motivated. It will help you develop relevant interesting content and allow you to find some early readers. They will help your work become successful.

After reading the chapter on marketing you'll be ready for the rest of the book. You will want to re-read the chapter on marketing after you are done writing your book.

Read on, and enjoy the life-affirming journey!

Chapter 2 Marketing your Book

You might find it strange to start this journey of creating a book with a chapter on how to market it, but "it's best to start with the end in mind," as our friend Steven Covey says.

Marketing your work is a big part of your journey. It intimidates many an author. Even writers signed to large publishing houses are obliged to do whatever they can to promote their own books.

Many different tactics exist for marketing a book. All of them operating together can help your cause: you can't only cherry-pick one, like Face-book. Sure, some people talk about social media as if creating a lead page will magically make you famous, but the internet is only one piece of the full marketing puzzle.

You can summarize the marketing of your book as "Building your Audience." It is not something that happens overnight.

If you are a social person, the marketing of your book might not be as hard as you think. However if you're a loner who has spent your free time reading rather than socializing, you are heading into a very large learning curve (see end of chapter for some tips). You should already have been an active member of the community for which you are writing. They should know you and respect you, and hopefully they have been supporting you throughout your book writing journey.

Where do you start building your audience? Start anywhere, but let's visit some likely venues.

1. Face to face meetings.

    Imagine a hypothetical *Time Management for Mothers* book. One potential meeting place would be a support group for mothers. The women in the club are there to raise their concerns, issues which could become content for your book. You are there listening, learning what your audience needs to know, so you can constantly make your book more and more relevant to them. Two great places to find a brick and mortar meeting place are Face-book and Meetup.com.

    Be creative with your search engine terms. To promote this book about time management for mothers of multiple births, you could join various mother support groups, working women's clubs, multiple birth clubs, and general interest women's support clubs. These groups will put you in touch with an audience with a keen interest in your topic. At these meetings, never start by pitching your book! Just meet people and create genuine relationships. No one likes being sold to, and it's important for you to create strong relationships with your first audience members. Your marketing can get a big boost later if you volunteer to help at upcoming events or if you run for a leadership position. Try to raise your profile in your budding community. It will help you to meet more and more members and to hear their concerns.

2. Becoming a speaker for meetings.

If you think an author can get away without speaking in public, you are crazy. You need to seek out speaking engagements to establish yourself as a valued member of the social circles to which your audience belongs. You don't have to wait until your book is completed. If your work is still in the oven, pass a sign-up sheet around the audience so you can send them info later. Add any potential readers to your mailing list. (See resources on mail list management.)

Make sure your speech gives your audience lots of content. If your speech is no more than publicity for your book, you will alienate your audience! Your speech should be tailored to your current audience, and include some current developments. The topic should be something very specific, maybe even a little controversial. In our *Time Management* example, an angle like "How does ObamaCare impact mothers of multiple births?" could generate interest, especially if you did not cover it in your book. At the same time, it will attract your audience. Good speeches can build your reputation as an expert, so that when people are seeking more information about your area, they will remember you and your book.

3. Speak at conferences.

You've built a nice audience in your home area. You are sure of the relevance of your material, and you are getting confident in your speaking abilities. Now it's time to go big! You can submit abstracts to upcoming conferences in your area. Start by doing an online search for conferences involving your subject. Make a list of any conferences calling for speakers along with the dates. Niche topics, of course, may not have conferences locally or anywhere else in the world. Realizing that an audience is hungry for your niche topic means you might want to start your own conference.

Abstracts (summaries) need to be submitted between three and nine months before a conference. Each event may have different speaker requirements. Some conferences do not publicly call for speakers at all. If not, contact the organizers to ask how to get included in the program. Yes, this is gutsy, but you've been bold enough to write a book already, so why not? Perfecting your abstract is critical. This is why knowing your audience and the culture of your audience is crucial. Hopefully the local leadership at your physical meetings will support you and help you revise your approach. They might even know someone in the leadership of the conference. When you do get to speak at a conference, have your books ready to sell at a table at the back of the room, assuming it is allowed by the organizers. If not, provide links or handouts which list your products. Make occasional reference to your book, but don't oversell it! If you can get your audience to sign up for your mailing list, do so. Also, if you can afford it, work with the conference organizers to use your book as a giveaway. It is a great tactic to get people talking about your book.

4. Marketing Materials.

Create a physical business card which features your book's name. It will help you meet people at events. Remember not to oversell! If your book happens to come up in conversation and they seem interested, give them a copy of the card.

Make flyers to hang in coffee shops or other spaces frequented by members of your audience. It is a long shot, but you can try.

You can also create short samples of your book, and print up related materials to give away. These should be enough to pique your audience's interest and get them to buy the full book. For example, for our *Time Management* book example, you could create a short, twenty page handbook called *Instant Shopping Lists for Mother's of Multiple Births*. That would be a useful reference. It helps establish you as an expert - and on the last page it will remind the reader that you have other helpful information in your excellent book.

5. Online Social Media.

Now let's talk about the other half of building your audience: working the online world. It is not about magic. You will need both the physical world and the online world working in harmony to be successful these days. After you've done real world events, you need to drive your new audience members to join your online audience by adding them to your mailing list, Twitter, LinkedIn, and Face-book. It's critical to keep in touch with your physical audience using such online methods. Your audience needs to be constantly reminded that you are the expert in this area.

a. You need to add any book contacts you make to your online social media networks.

b. Join some Face-book and LinkedIn groups located in your area. They can become as important to building your audience as any physical groups. Continue to interact and network with those you meet online. Find out what is on their minds!

c. Make a Face-book and/or LinkedIn page for you and for your book. I would make one for each book you want to market.

d. There is no shortcut to networking. If you feel this is all too hard or too much effort, you are probably out of luck. You will need to post frequently. You need to share interesting content. Your content should derive from your interactions with members of your audience. You are creating real relationships with potential buyers, just like you did at the physical meetings. Ask them friendly questions. What are they worried about? What do they think is funny? How can you keep giving them things they want to read and hear? What items in the news have they heard that you should be aware of?

6. Web Pages/Blogs.

Ahh, the book web page. Do you need one? Maybe. It can't hurt to register a domain name that is the name of your book, if it is available. Nowadays you might just want to have a domain that points to a blog or a Face-book page, if possible. A blog on a major site such as WordPress or Blogger will allow a domain name (ie *MothersofMultipleBirths.com*) to be redirected to a page on their site.

Having a blog is a great place to post thoughts, news, and controversial stories to help your audience stay interested in you, the expert! You can set up your blog page with a box (form) to capture email addresses of web surfers who want to stay connected with you. Make sure they "Opt In" to your mailing list. You don't want to be accused of spamming. Also don't use your own email address, since spam bots might pick it up and spam you. Give a prize, e.g. a free chapter, in exchange for a reader entering his or her email address. Email your blog contacts about upcoming speaking events or any new books you are writing. You can also auto-sign them up for an email campaign, whereby you send them highly interesting content on a regular basis so they will not forget you.

7. Newsletters/Daily emails.

A lot of authors send out a monthly newsletter or a "daily quote" to keep their audience engaged. You can post such content to Face-book or LinkedIn as well. Keep your messages/articles relevant and interesting.

8. Guest Blogging.

Guest writing on another person's blog is a great way to build your audience. The blog in question should already be popular with your target audience and should allow you to link back to your own blog or Face-book page.

9. Podcasting.

People love podcasts because they can listen while on the go. (See the references for information on podcasting.) Always drive the audience back to your blog or Face-book page so that you can continue to interact with them

Remember that the physical and online worlds need to work in tandem. Research shows that face-to-face relationships have a stronger impact than online only. Nonetheless, if the initial connection was created face-to-face, the follow-up interactions online can still be impactful. (A great book to learn more about this effect is *Social Physics* by Alex "Sandy" Pentland.)

Over and over I will remind you to create meaningful, real relationships. Craft interesting, relevant content. There are no short cuts to building an audience. It takes time. The more you put yourself out there and stay visible online, the more successful your career as an author can be.

If you're a very shy introverted artist, here are some tips for getting comfortable with the physical meetings:

1. Read a book on conversation

    This may seem so basic, yet a book can give you ideas on how to start a conversation with a complete stranger. Mostly it's about asking questions and listening carefully.

2. Get an extroverted buddy to go with you to meetings, someone to stroll with around the room

    You know who you can drag with you. Tell them how important this is to you. Ask them to stand by your side so you can make some new friends. Once you have made a few new connections and friendships you can set your wingman free.

3. Join Toastmasters

    Toastmasters is a safe, friendly environment where you can get used to talking in public. The format makes it easy to make connections. Go to Toastmasters.org for local club listings.

4. Take an improv class

    Taking an improv class will build your confidence, so you feel at ease in your skin. It will teach you how to trust in your first instincts, to be both an attentive listener and a fast thinker. Try to find a drop-in class in your area by googling it.

5. Get a hug from a friend before you enter the social event

    When you get a hug, it releases hormones which flush out the stress hormone, cortisol. You will feel more relaxed before you even enter the meeting.

6. Standup straight and tall and hold your head up high

    Your posture also affects your hormone levels. Standing up straight and holding your head up high can also flush out stress.

Chapter 3 Plan

Come up with a topic

What to write about?

For some this decision is hard. There are just too many topics out there! For others it might be a hard call, because it seems that everything subject has been written about already. For me it is the former issue. If you have too few ideas, make a list of topics about which you are passionate. If you have too many ideas, write the list of topics you know very well. Then prioritize which topics you should write about first.

Now that you have a list, start to narrow your topic. See how many books are already written on your subject. Would yours be the first one? Maybe that's because it's not a topic anyone would find interesting (e.g. the thankfully-never-written book, Dog Poop Flower Arranging Techniques). If there aren't any books on the subject, try doing a poll on Face-book or LinkedIn to see if anyone else thinks it's worth writing. It would be a shame if you wrote a book and did not sell any copies!

If there are many books on the subject, definite interest already exists (witness the very popular topic of Time Management). The danger of writing within a popular genre is, of course, that your topic may already be saturated. All your hard work might get lost like a needle in the haystack of books already available.

You can overcome this by finding a unique, specialized Point of View, such as Time Management for Busy Working Mothers of Triplets. You'll be creating a niche market within which you could have a best seller. (You may have to weed out readers who only have twins, however.)

Use this Venn diagram to see where you would have optimal focus:

Figure 1: Use this Venn diagram to decide where to focus your book.

I dug deep for mine: How to become a Software Architect. When I wanted to become a software architect, no one could tell me how to do it. I searched Amazon for a "How To", but there wasn't one. Yet I was seeing many books on software architecture, so I knew there was a market. I polled colleagues of mine about the idea of writing such a book, and all were very encouraging.

Write an outline

An outline is a map that you create. You will often rewrite it, even as you are following it.

Start by brainstorming all the possible subtopics under your main title. Don't worry about the order: just write! Sit with a friend, throw out ideas, and write all of them down.

Once you have a nice list of ideas, review it with trusted colleagues. Organize it into chapters. Don't get stuck reordering, though; it is easy to get stuck reorganizing this list again and again. When I wrote my book, I changed my outline many times.

As you write, you may discover that your writing is not sticking to the plan. You might be inspired to go in a totally different direction! Or, you might realize that the first few chapters would make a great book on their own if they were lifted out and expanded – which unfortunately means you may end up trashing all the leftover chapters!

Make a schedule

Writing on a schedule does not sound very artistic, but it may be the only way to compel you to finish your book!

Your writing schedule will be part of a timeline. Remember that editing, post production, and promotion are on that timeline also, so you will need to be disciplined if you want to get a first draft of your book written quickly. Try on the mindset that you must get the first draft done within x days/months. Then you will turn to re-writing and editing.

For the first nine months of my timeline, I only wrote on airplanes, which was hardly ideal. In September 2011, I realized I needed to get more serious about my book. So I made a schedule. I forced myself to write 700 words every weekday morning, and the system worked!

Now and then as you write, monitor your word count meter. Don't quit for the day until you've met your quota. An e-book should be between 35k and 50k words. Consumers don't seem to buy a paper book unless it has at least 300 pages, so many print authors actually pad out their short books with repetition and filler. However, digital books can be any length you want.

Choose a deadline for your draft.

Select a target for your total word count.

Work backwards to figure out how many words you need to write a day. Do you want to write every day, or only on workdays? Will you only be writing on the weekend? (I am a book coach. The hardest discussions with my clients are about free time: no one ever has any!)

Writing as a profession is a significant time commitment. Accept this and make the necessary sacrifices. Look at your weekly obligations. What can you skip for a few months in order to make room for writing? How important is being an author to you? If it's not that important, it is possible that it won't ever happen. If it really means a lot to you, you should schedule it in, just as you would a critical appointment. Honor yourself by honoring your goal. Treat it as the top priority that it deserves to be.

Before each scheduled writing session, turn off or remove all unhelpful distractions, including the internet and cell phones. If you have family members who require your attentions, work out an arrangement with them.

For my novel, Engineer Your Perfect Child, my target word count was 50k. I decided to have my draft finished in thirty days. Therefore I vowed to write 1667 words every morning for the next month, in the early hours. I asked my husband and live-in sister not to talk to me or distract me in any way during these crucial times. Throughout the month, they did often try to interrupt anyway, but I had to remind them that I needed to focus!

Every weekday I wrote, per my schedule. On the weekends, I thought I would be squeezing in some more time – at least that was the plan. I discovered however that, even if I was relatively free on a Saturday or a Sunday, I'd end up procrastinating and not writing at all. And that was because I wasn't sticking to the routine. So I recommend that serious authors maintain a consistent daily writing schedule, whenever possible.

Chapter 4 Write

In order to make it easier to publish later, use standard Word formatting for headers and paragraphs.

Don't expect to write a perfect first draft. Be patient with yourself. Keep in mind the oft repeated saying, "perfect is the enemy of done". The secret to writing a great book is to write regularly: your butt in the seat; your fingers on the keyboard. You do need to type the words out. Wannabe authors dream and procrastinate. Real authors actually write sentences and paragraphs!

Some authors write prolifically, while others can't think of anything to write because they need to be "inspired" first. I believe that waiting for inspiration is a myth; it is not something any serious writer would advocate. Writing is a discipline, not just an art.

Every book you have ever read started with one word, but don't get stuck on crafting the perfect first sentence. Get a flow going. Also, don't worry too much about word choice. You can change out words later during editing. With your outline as a guide, start any of the chapters that seem easiest.

Let's discuss some techniques to help get you writing.

- Find an appropriate soundtrack, if it is not too distracting.
- Google a quote. Then think about what that quote means to your subject. Do you agree or disagree? Do you have a relevant anecdote from your life you could share?
- Readers enjoy personal stories. Think about your current chapter. Has anything hit the news recently on this subject that you could write about? How about a personal childhood memory? Flip through your journal or blog for related material. Pull out a book you read recently on the subject. Just start writing!
- Some exercises that other writers have found useful in revving their engine: "I am sitting here with my coffee. It's too hot to drink, so I am just smelling it." Only after words have started to flow, do you steer yourself toward your subject. For example, "When I discovered I was pregnant with triplets, I had to lay off the coffee. I was very sad at first. But having three wonderful babies makes me glad that I quit..."

Hemingway always left a sentence incomplete at the end of a writing session. That way, he would know how he was going to start writing the next time.

Once your words are flowing, you should be set. Keep writing until you hit your word count. I set up my writing program so that the word count displayed at the bottom of my screen:

Page: 10 of 13 | Words: 2,732

Figure 2: Keep the Word Count at the bottom of your screen.

Stick to your schedule, but forgive yourself if you miss your target. It's really not the end of the world!

You can keep motivated by finding yourself a writing buddy or writing accountability partner, and/or a writing club.

When you team up with a writing buddy daily you can keep each other focused, whether online or in person. If no writing buddy is available, try an accountability partner, a person you report to daily with your word count. You can also post your word count on Face-book or Twitter to stay motivated.

Writing clubs can be energizing. In Tampa we have "Novel Writing Pods", as part of the Tampa Writers Alliance. Each pod has only four or five members. The pods meet regularly to track each other's progress and to hear each other's work. Check with your local writing clubs to see if they have similar work groups in your area.

National Novel Writing Month is a worldwide event every November. It is a huge challenge. NaNoWriMo Members write 1667 words a day in order to have drafted a complete novel in one month. Like many, I used it to keep me on track. Each day I posted my word count. The NaNoWriMo website creates a personalized chart for you that looks like this:

Figure 3: National Novel Writing Month allows you to track your progress.

Even after NaNoWriMo was over, I used their method to help me write the sequel to my first novel. I monitored my daily output with my own chart. (In the Resources section of this book you can find printable, customizable versions of such charts.)

My point is: do whatever it takes to keep yourself motivated enough to complete your book.

Don't forget to back up your book by emailing it to yourself daily. I've known people who lost everything they had written after a computer crash. What could be more depressing! And long before the digital age, Hemingway lost all of his writing once. Don't be a loser!

(If you are planning an audiobook, writing short chapters will prove helpful in managing the files later on. Read the Publish Audio section to get more insight into audiobooks.)

Chapter 5 Editing

You've finished the first draft: it's time to do the hard part. The editing!

One of my writing friends told me, "All writing is rewriting." For many, rewriting is a difficult phase in the creation of a book.

First, reread your chapters and, as you go, fix any overall composition or flow issues. For fiction, it's good to rewrite your book's outline so as to keep your plot straight. You might need to fix some continuity issues. If your book is non-fiction, review the overall composition and layout, and reorder your work as needed. Review the overall flow with trusted friends or colleagues to see if it really is the best layout. Try different flows to see if one is better than another. (Perfect is still the enemy of done, however.)

If enough people tell you that your current layout is confusing, you better change it. If only one person has an issue, though, she might just be having a bad day!

The next level of fine tuning is to look for inconsistencies in your chapters. For instance, say each chapter starts with a personal story before an in-depth discussion, but you notice that a couple of your chapters are the other way around. Make them consistent across: readers will enjoy the pattern.

Check out your paragraph structures. Make sure you are covering one idea in each paragraph. If you find that you have several ideas jammed into one paragraph, make separate paragraphs. Watch for the flow of the paragraphs. Is there another arrangement that makes more sense?

How are your sentence structures? Stick to active voice, avoiding passive "being" verbs like "is" and "are." I will give you an example: "Mistakes were made." Vs. "I, the president, totally lied, cheated and stole." You can see the passive voice vs. the active voice. Not all sentences need to be active, but where you can, you should try to use it.

Think about word choice. You want to make your ideas clear without overwhelming your readers with your prodigious, erudite vocabulary. Use fun alliteration, like "I never expected labor to be easy, but the surgeon performed a straightforward, simple, and safe c-section." Readers enjoy this type of sentence, because of the three parallel words starting with the letter 's'. (For more fine tuning of sentences, read Strunk and White's wonderful little book, The

Elements of Style. My Resources appendix has further recommendations for grammar handbooks.)

Once you have honed your chapters, paragraphs, and sentences, send your draft to your most trusted friends. Ask them to tell you if it has any hope of becoming an interesting book. Look for honest feedback, not flattery. Enclose a short questionnaire with the manuscript of your book. Here is the poll I sent along with my software architecture book:

Did you finish reading the book?

Rate 1-10 the interest level you felt. 1 - not very interested; 10 - very interested.

Which chapters did you like the best?

What other chapters do you wish I had included?

Any comments?

The answers to such a questionnaire will help you hone in on the parts that need work. Spend more time refining those areas of the text.

Once you've incorporated feedback from your first readers into your draft, run through the steps above again. Re-inspect your chapters, paragraphs, and sentences. Often when you change your text you will accidentally introduce new errors! Those too will need correcting.

Assuming you've re-written your book once or twice, it's time to seek professional help. Don't employ an editor until you've advanced your book as far as you possibly can on your own. Be patient until you are ready: after all, editors cost money.

How do you find an editor? Ask your local writing club for references. Look on Google, Face-book, and LinkedIn. Can other authors recommend a competent editor? Some writers do editing on the side. If you've been networking properly, you can line up a few editors to interview. It's great when you find one who is all about your type of writing. Some editors specialize in fiction, others non-fiction; some will tackle either. If your topic is highly technical, try to find yourself an editor as near to your field as possible.

The editor-author relationship is a very special one. It can only help if you have chemistry and trust with your editor. Interview a few of them to see how the relationship feels. Ask them about previous work they've done. Figure out how much you are willing to pay. Show them a sample to see if they are at all interested. They may demand a more drastic level of re-writing before even taking you on.

Once you've selected your editor, determine a new timeline for your book. Decide how often editing feedback or questions should be sent back and forth, and be committed to responding quickly to the editor's comments and questions. Remember, your collaborator can't more forward without your responses.

You'll need to stay flexible when you listen to critiques. It is likely an editor will give you some painful feedback! Writers tend to fall in love with their words, while editors are hired to prune. Hemingway once said that a writer should be judged by the quality of the writing that gets cut.

Cut, rewrite, rethink...

You may have to go back and forth for a while. Editing my novel took six months. I used two editors, plus several friends as reviewers.

Once you get your draft back from the editor, give it a thorough read to ensure that the book still flows as you expect it to, or better. Send copies out to another set of friends, along with a questionnaire to see if you've lost them along the way. Most likely you will need a separate set of friends for this round: few will care to read the same book twice in a row, no matter how much they love you. Incorporate any feedback, then do one more fine comb read-through.

Title

You have settled on a final title. If not: what are you waiting for? Do it! Picking a title can be the difficult. I recommend you survey friends to help decide. You could check key words on Google and see which costs the most. This indicates how much they are being searched for. I recommend a straight forward title. If it is a novel you might want to use that in the subtitle. I have some issues with my title of my novel *Engineer Your Perfect Child.* People think it's a parenting book, as terrifying as that sounds. Let's say you have two working titles, you can do A/B testing which means you can create a Google ad and see which generates more clicks.

Chapter 6 Cover, Illustrations and Formatting

It is time to work on the graphics: your book cover, and any illustrations you have in mind. I recommend you find a professional artist, one whom you trust. Expect to pay what they are worth! No matter what they say, everyone judges a book by its cover. Have your artist make several versions that are very different. Poll your friends to check out their reactions, maybe even do a Face-book or LinkedIn survey. Compare it to the covers of other books in your field. Go by what feels right to you, but also rely on the good judgment of your artist. Bounce a few covers off your editor to see what he or she thinks. If worst comes to worst, you can use Kindle and Create Space to create a cover.

Don't dither. Pick one cover and commit to it! You'll never make everyone happy no matter which version you choose.

Then insert the cover graphic into the first page of your Word document.

If your book has illustrations, you can sketch them yourself or make notes about what you need. To create your illustrations, hire the same graphic artist or find another. Be sure to number all your images and subtitle them correctly. Word gives you an easy way to manage illustrations through captions: when you right-click on one, go to Insert Caption and fill out the box.

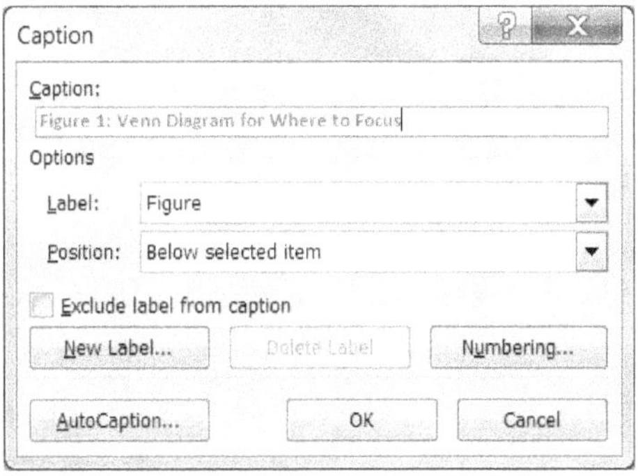

Figure 4: Use Word's Caption system.

Older Kindle e-readers do not have color. You can use grayscale for any illustrations that don't require color. You will be paying for the bandwidth used during downloads of your e-book. An e-book with large graphics will cost you, the author, more per download. A manuscript with color images will cost more to print, so carefully consider if it is the right choice for you.

Use standard Word formatting for headers and paragraphs. Use Heading 1 style for chapter titles, then insert a Reference-> Table of Contents:

Figure 5: Use Word's Table of Contents.

To format your manuscript for Kindle, use normal Word formatting. Kindle Publishing uses the Table of Contents to create a set of links at the beginning of your book to help your reader navigate. You might need to remove any extra spaces between paragraphs which are making your pages look empty. The Kindle viewer allows you to review your e-book after you upload it. You may have to tweak the file online to get it looking right. Make sure each chapter starts at the top of the page. Use Insert-> "Page Break", so that chapters don't start in the middle of a page.

Add page numbers.

Bett Correa

Click the "Options" Section, under the "Design Tab", click on "Different First Page". otherwise a page number will show up right on your book cover! Delete extra space between the tops of the pages and the chapter titles.

Chapter 7 Publish

Kindle Publishing

E-books or electronic books are all the rage nowadays. Readers can carry hundreds of them on their smartphone or tablet.

For those who are confused about what Kindle Publishing means: you do not need to have in hand the physical Kindle device from Amazon.com. Free Kindle Apps and Kindle Readers are available to install on all smartphones, tablets, laptops, and desktops. You can go online, download this app from Amazon, and have Kindle books sent to your device in minutes.

Amazon makes publishing to this format very easy. The Nook version is not so easy to use. Barnes & Noble keeps a tight rein on which authors can publish through them.

People often ask me about publishing in other e-book formats, such as ePub. I don't see any reason to.

If your goal is to make your book available without the hassle of selling it, you can simply save your book as a PDF and post it straight to your blog or website. If you want to get paid for all your efforts, you (or a web designer) can build an author website with a shopping cart that incorporates Paypal or one of the other credit card processing services. Using such web carts, you collect your payment and then email the e-book directly to your customer or send back a secret hyperlink to your manuscript file.

Frankly, I feel the personal website option is too much work. I use Kindle because:

1. Amazon.com is the world's largest bookseller.
2. Amazon takes care of everything: your shopping cart, your cataloging and inventory, as well as distribution.
3. Kindle offers you protection from piracy.

I recommend you create yourself an Amazon account. It doesn't cost you anything to set up, you don't need to pay anyone to do it for you, and you can have it up yourself very quickly. It only took me a few minutes to fill out the information. You do not even need an ISDN number to publish your book. Here's how it works:

Create a New Title. Fill in all the metadata about your book, including your author name under 'Contributors'.

Upload your Word document, including the front cover graphic which you inserted into the first page of the document. The upload might take a few minutes depending on the length of your book. Preview the book and see how it looks in the online Kindle simulator.

At this point you may find that spacing and picture alignment have drifted off. Simply go back to the Word document, keep editing and re-uploading until you get it looking right.

Don't forget the page numbering!

Figure 6: Add a New Title.

Select your royalties model. They are two options: 35% royalty for books priced between $.99 and $200; 70% royalty for books between $2.99 and $9.99.

You must deciding how much to charge for your own work. Some artists believe that no price would be high enough for their precious work, while others totally undervalue their work. Is it better to sell for cheaper while you are building an audience? It makes sense, yet some judge a work's value mainly by its price tag, so pricing it higher will be better. You need to research the market and ask your trusted friends what they think is fair.

You're done! Click 'Publish'!

It takes twelve hours for Kindle to process your book and make it available to download. If you find any further issues you can always update the document, or any of the metadata, after the twelve hours is up. During that time window, all the links for editing your book are grayed out.

Figure 7: Amazon takes 12 hours to process your book.

Figure 8: Amazon takes 12 hours to process your book.

Paper Publishing

A few readers in the world still enjoy holding a paper book in their hands. For them, you can create a print version of your new book using Create Space, which is also owned by Amazon. The reason I used Create Space is because it shows the book on amazon.com alongside your Kindle version and it is Print on Demand. This means Create Space only prints a book once someone orders it. The printed book is more complicated to create, for a few reasons.

First, you will need to order a 'proof version', a single copy of the book, before your work can be made available to the public. The proof will take several days to ship, and you must pay for this. Formatting for print is trickier than for digital-only.

I'll walk you through the Create Space publishing steps with screenshots. Let's jump in!

On the Createspace.com website, click Sign Up.

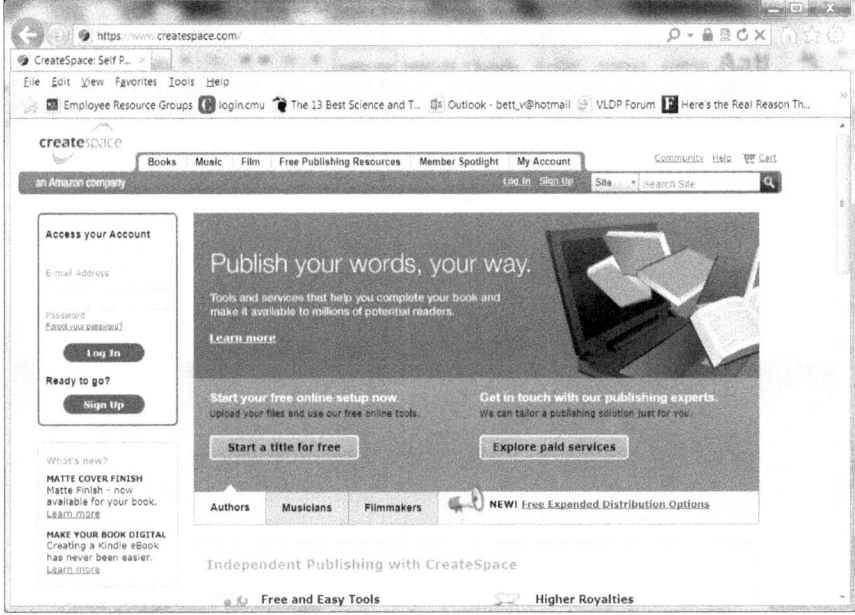

Figure 9: CreateSpace.com home page.

Step by Step: Write, Self-publish, and Market Your Book

Enter the email address you use with your amazon.com account.

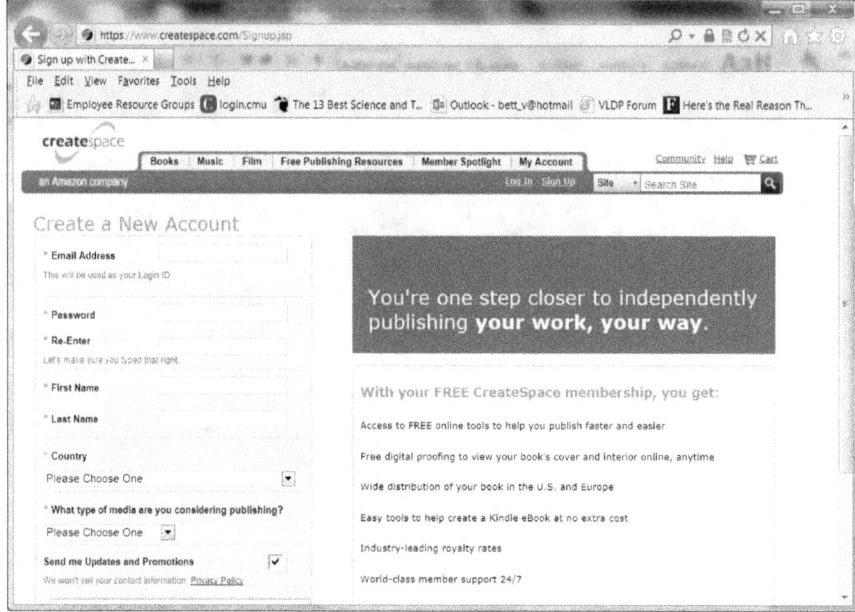

Figure 10: CreateSpace.com signup page.

Click Create new Title.

Bett Correa

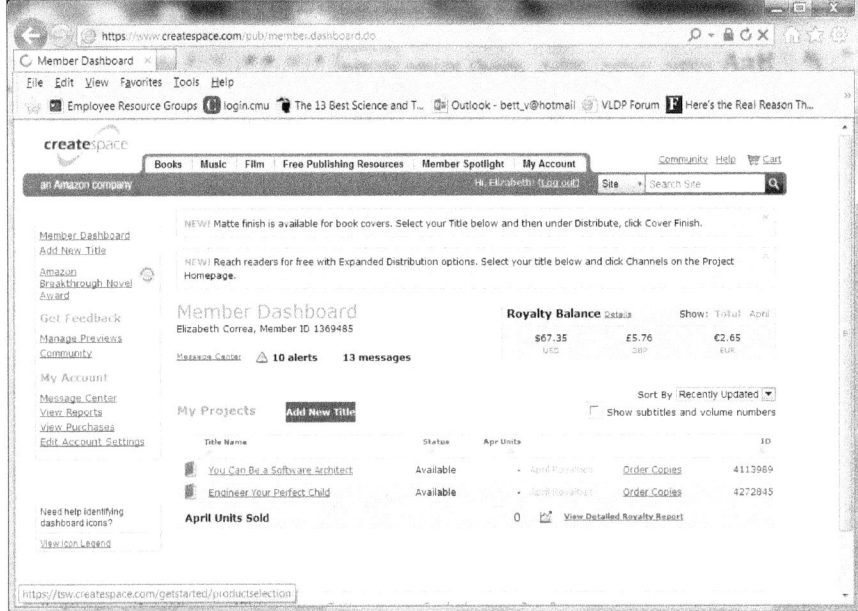

Figure 11: CreateSpace.com dashboard page.

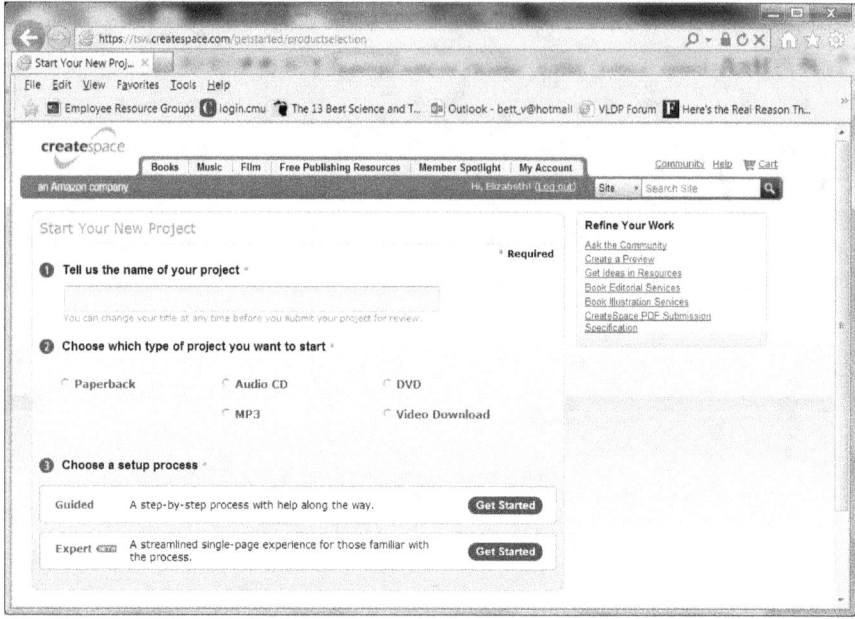

Figure 12: CreateSpace.com Start Your New Project page.

The coloring of your book and its page dimensions are important factors that you need to weigh carefully. Color printing within your book will cost you more out of pocket, and it will raise the selling price of your book. You will probably have a color book cover graphic, however.

Bett Correa

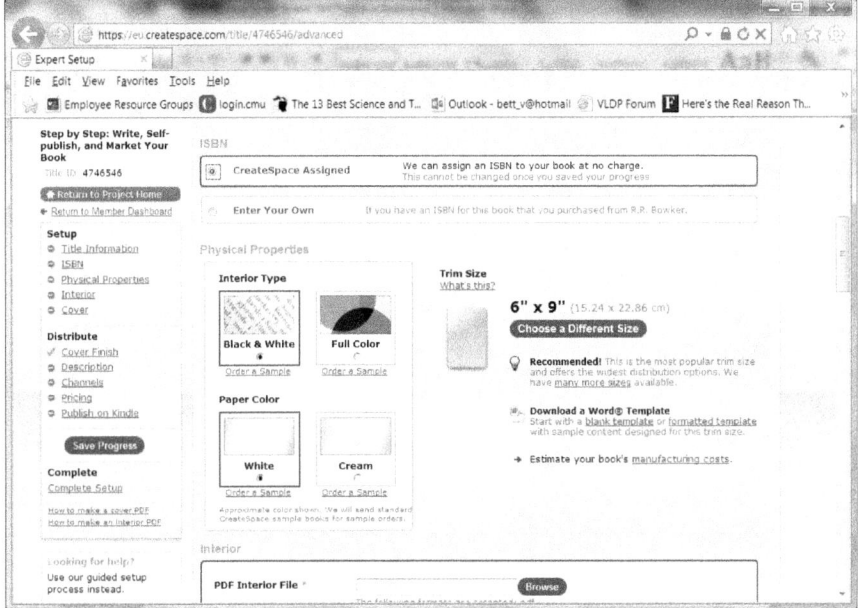

Figure 13: CreateSpace.com book formatting page.

You will need to save your Word document as a PDF version. Upload the PDF to Create Space.

Figure 14: CreateSpace.com cover creator page.

Preview the book online. Verify the page numbering, image positioning, borders, and the general look of the book. Is it up to your standards of quality?

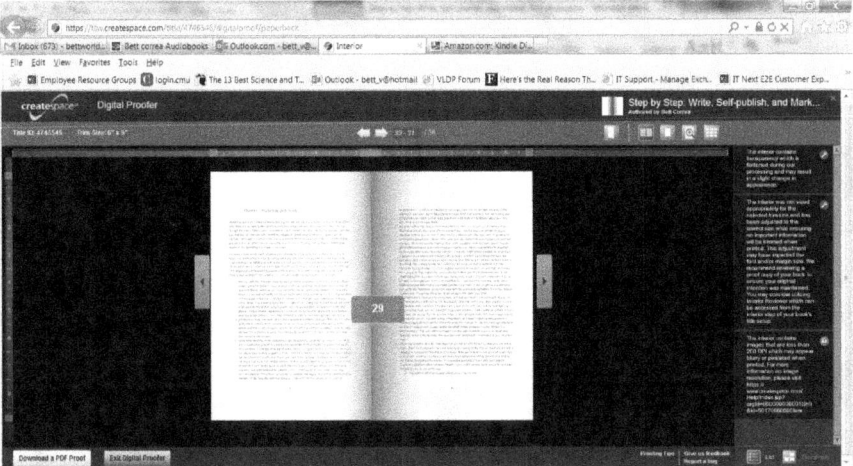

Figure 15: Createspace.com Digital Proofer.

Cover

One of the more complex features of your printed book is the cover graphic. Unlike the Kindle e-version, the printed cover graphic will also need to include the designs for your spine and back cover. The width of the spine is based on the number of pages in your book. You will need to communicate with your graphic artist about this. The Create Space website will calculate the necessary dimensions for your book spine. You can check the results in their previewing system. The back cover should look as professional as the front, with quotes, a blurb about the contents, and maybe a photo of you the author. Don't forget to leave room in the back cover graphic where your barcode will be inserted…

You've gone a few rounds of reformatting. Your Word document is fixed, and you've uploaded the revised PDF. You are proofing the hard copy that Create Space sent you. Make sure the margins are consistent. I know I had a lot of images that ran over the edges of the page.

Once the proof copy looks good, you can approve it in the Create Space form online. Now, at long last, you can order a few copies and give them to your parents and friends, or anyone who helped you edit. Make sure you sign your gifts! ☺

Order a number of copies for marketing your work. (See the chapters on Marketing for more details.)

Audio Version

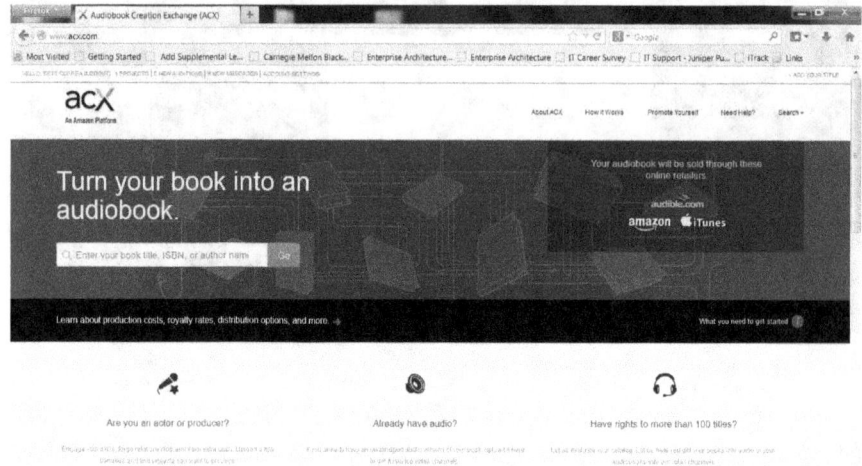

Figure 16: acx.com home page.

Audiobooks have a reputable history. The unrefuted source we call Wikipedia says that they were first available in the 1930's. I am sure some senior readers remember listening to books on LP players or on cassette tape. Many audiobooks are currently available on CD.

More recently, Amazon.com has made it easier for all of us to consume audiobooks by creating Audbile.com, an audiobook file downloading site. People on the go who enjoy books can digest a downloaded audiobook in a few days while they are commuting or exercising. Audible has created a subscription model whereby, for a low fee, customers receive one book a month. Its customers can listen to e-books on their smartphones, or download them to their computer, or burn copies of them onto CD-Rs.

Frankly, creating an audio version of your book can be just as challenging as the actual writing! You will need a narrator to do the voice acting and to record/produce the results. You have several options:

1. Use the central agency, ACX.com, to find a narrator.

Pros: When you request a narrator through ACX, you fill out a form about what type of narrator you want (i.e. Male, Female, Midwest, Southern, etc). Narrators can message you back through the site and send you mp3 auditions. You will need to pay for this, and we will cover a few payment options.

Cons: The downside to using ACX to find a narrator is that the site then owns the full rights to your audiobook. If you don't go through ACX, you own the rights to your work. You can read through the legalese and talk to friends with firsthand experience in order to decide which option is right for you.

2. Locate a professional narrator yourself.

Pros: You will retain the copyright to your audiobook. You can select an actor friend, or use a personal recommendation, which will hopefully ensure the quality you want.

Cons: Not everyone has a friend network full of talented narrators! If you don't operate within such circles, go to ACX or record the audiobook yourself.

3. Narrate the book yourself.

Pros: It's cheap, and you retain the full copyright.

Cons: You sound like you! You had better love the sound of your own voice… and the results may sound as cheap as the audio gear on which you recorded.

Think about these three options when you create your ACX audiobook account. You'll use your Amazon.com account to sign up.

Figure 17: acx.com uses amazon.com for signin page.

Although ACX tries to make your life easy, they can be confusing. You will need to "claim" your book, but you need to have already published your book on Kindle for it to work. You should see your book listed when you log in. Click "This is My Book."

Bett Correa

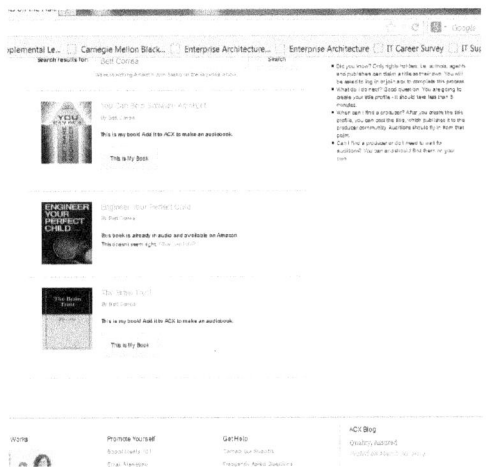

Figure 18: acx.com "This is My Book" page.

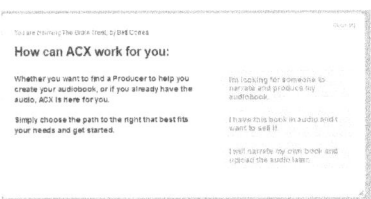

Figure 19: acx.com has three options for publishing audio books.

Let's look at your 3 audiobook options:

1. Use ACX.com to find a narrator

Figure 20: acx.com agreement for hiring a narrator.

2. Hire a professional narrator yourself and

3. Narrate the book yourself

You will need to decide if you want to sign an exclusive contract with ACX. It will give you major distribution through Audible, iTunes, and Amazon. Their exclusive contract gives you 40% of the royalties. Their non-exclusive contract only pays a 25% royalty, however it lets you sell your audiobook not just on the three big sites but anywhere else you choose. I selected 'Exclusive' because I know most people get their books from those three stores - plus it's a higher percentage royalty.

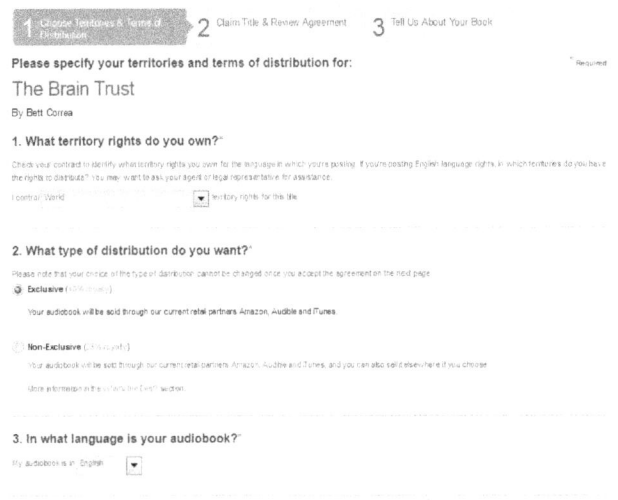

Figure 21: acx.com upload your own audio book option.

Take time to think about these business decisions. Consult any friends who know more about audiobooks and can give you guidance about your specific case.

Once you've signed your contract with ACX, you can move forward and take the following steps:

1. If you've decided to let ACX help you record your book, you'll need to spend time listening to narrator auditions. Finalize which narrator you want.

2. If you've hired a narrator yourself, you will need to work together on the production. For my sci-fi novel I took this option. I already knew my narrator from the improv scene to which we both belong in Tampa. He had lots of experience doing fiction narration and was happy to do mine. My book was especially challenging because I had set it in Peru, with scenes in China and in the U.S., and he had to do all the accents for both male and female characters. Don't write books with such complications if you want to save money on your audiobook!

Working with your narrator can take as much time again as writing your book. You'll need to help your narrator navigate through ACX if they've not used it before. (See below for how to format the files.)

3. If you've decided to narrate the book yourself, you are going to need a lot more help than I can offer in this handbook. (I've included a link in the resources section of the book.) Here are a few tips I've learned from my own network of voice actors:
    a. Find a small enclosed area to record
    b. Cover the walls with blankets
    c. Use a good mic
    d. Edit using Audacity, which is a simple-to-use freeware program
    e. After making mp3s for upload to ACX, don't delete your masters, i.e. your high quality WAV files. You never know when they might be needed again!

A discussion of Audio Formatting

If you did not select an ACX narrator, you need to be very careful about the audio formatting of the book. Mono recording, not stereo recording is recommended in the ACX guidelines.

Your narrator should record a simple intro for your audiobook. ACX gives you the required format for this introductory mp3:

Opening
[Title]
Written by [Your name]
Narrated by [Your narrator's name]

Closing Credits:
This has been [Title]
Written by [Your name]

Narrated by [Your narrator's name]

Copyright [20xx and your name]

Production copyright [20xx] by [Your name]

Chapters

Each chapter needs a separate audio file. It's easiest when your chapters are short, because the audio files will stay a manageable size. You can use Drop Box or Google Drive to transfer files between you and the narrator. You need to record the mp3s at the highest quality possible. The mp3 bit rate required is 192Kbps. Each chapter of audio needs to have 3.5 seconds of silence at the end. (In the resources section of this book, find links to the full audio requirements. I highly recommend you read them fully before embarking on this tricky journey.)

You've assembled all your audio chapters, including the opening and closing files. Now you are ready to upload the files, one by one, onto the website.

The cover artwork for the audiobook requires different dimensions from your book in Kindle or Create Space. The ACX graphic has to be square, like a CD cover. I used my artist's PSD files to create a square version. You won't be able to change the artwork after you publish your audiobook, so make sure you are very happy with it!

This is the easiest part of the whole process. Once you've uploaded all the audio and graphic files, the ACX team should approve your production within twenty one days. They will email you a notification that your book is now ready for purchase on Audible.com.

For weeks I kept searching for my name on Audible, and the day the news arrived I was overjoyed!

Step by Step: Write, Self-publish, and Market Your Book

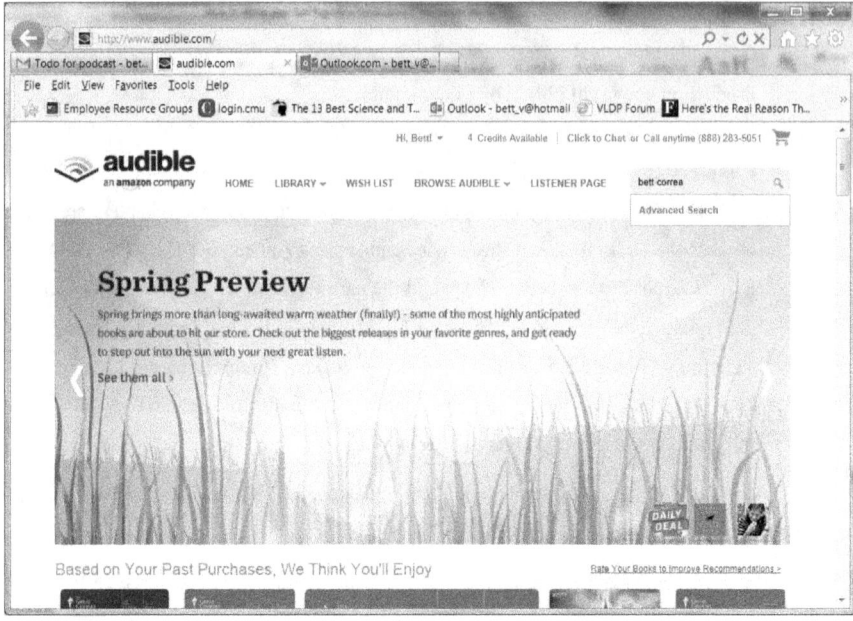

Figure 22: audible.com home page.

Bett Correa

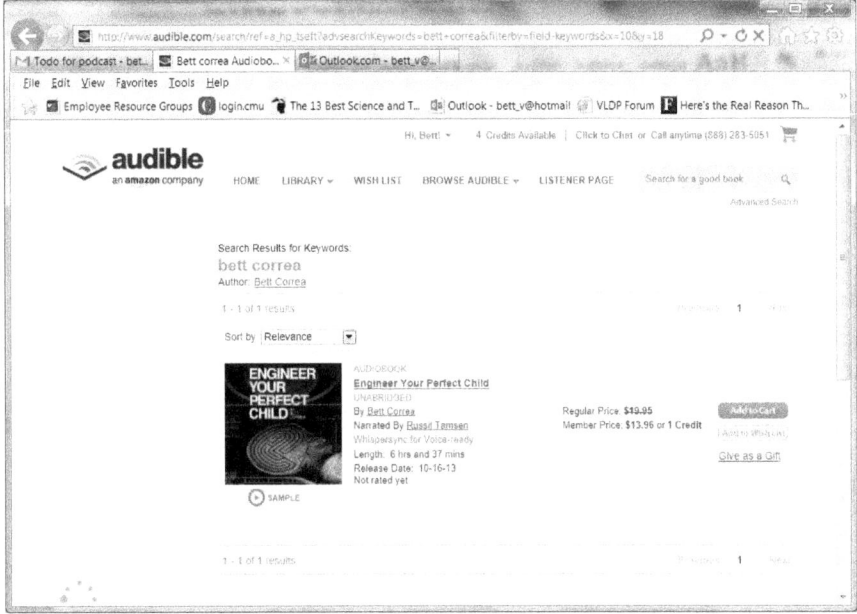

Figure 23: audible.com Engineer Your Perfect Child search results.

Seeing your audiobook for sale on Audible.com will be a very happy day for you too…

But your timeline is not over yet. Now you need to market your book and audiobook!

Chapter 8 Conclusion

Building your audience is an ongoing effort. Your first book shouldn't be your last! As you interact with your fans and learn what worries or excites them, you continue to create content that interests them. Go explore the world. Find new ways of expressing all the exciting things which you are discovering; figure out new ways to inspire your audience! Writing a book is one way to live an exciting and fulfilling life, although it's most likely not a way to become wealthy fast. You will probably need to continue to earn money in other ways. Still, being an author will enrich your life, as well as those of your readers.

I have loved writing and publishing my own work. I really enjoy interacting with my audience. Whatever reasons you have to write a book, I hope that it will be a life-affirming journey... and I hope you keep in touch with me!

Chapter 9 Resources

Books I recommend on the fine art of writing

On Writing by Sol Stein

On Writing by Steven King

The Elements of Style by Strunk and White

Work book for tracking your progress

http://www.silverage-books.pwp.blueyonder.co.uk/mag/ns/issues/NS2007.pdf

Audio Book help

http://www.acx.com/help/acx-audio-submission-requirements/200485520

This link is for Podcasting, but the information is also great for a first time narrator

http://www.hanselman.com/blog/HowToStartYourFirstPodcastEquipmentEditingPublishingAndMore.aspx

Mail List Management

I use Mailchimp for my mail list management. It is easy to use and free. I create a paper form with the "Opt In" request clearly spelled out, for example "To get updates from Bett, include your email address and name."

Should you Self Publish? Here are some comments from Book publisher and   publishing coach named Jewel Parago of Evershinepress.com

> Traditional vs. Self-Publishing – this is a choice the author should take time to consider. The author can easily traditionally publish through Indie publishers bypassing the "big six" publishers (Random House, Simon & Shuster, etc.). Making the choice to self-publish means that the author is going to become the publisher and many authors who go this route never learn half of what this means or what the major decisions are that need to be made prior to publishing. It is not true that anything can be fixed later. Depending upon the author's goals will determine whether getting the book into established distribution channels will be important. The main stream distribution market does not like or in some cases allow Amazon and other self-publishing platforms into their distribution

channels. This decision also determines if the author needs to purchase their own ISBN number, as they will not be able to Amazon's even the so-called customized numbers.

Jewel also has a few other comments that I think are important to consider on pricing, format and the importance of reviews

Price is a very important factor with customers. Avid readers who buy a lot of books consider the price of the books they buy as a determining factor. Amazon free days can be an incentive for avid readers to pick up books during the free days, however authors need to determine whether the exclusivity required to get the 70% royalty and free days are in fact worth it if the book cannot be listed with other vendors. Authors should realize that Amazon is a business and are looking out for themselves. They offer some good benefits to authors as a means to promote and induce sales for Amazon. Some of the exposure and sales may trickle down to the author, but Amazon's main focus is what is good for Amazon. For novice authors unsure of the publishing marketplace don't have a problem with the exclusivity and benefit from it. Authors looking for a broader marketplace and audience use Amazon only as another retailer in a field of many retailers and seek marketing and reviews that can apply to all retail avenues.

Ebooks – unless Amazon is going to be the author's only retail venue then they should focus on creating the epub version of the book first. Epub is the standardized digital format that all ebook platforms use. Once the epub files are created the author can upload the epub file to Amazon for conversion to the Kindle format. Epub files covert better to Kindle than word documents plus the author already has the correct file type to convert to the Apple iTunes format and Mobi or use as is for Nook and most others.

Chapter 10 About the Author

Figure 24: Bett Correa.

Bett Correa, author of two books, professional public speaker, Distinguished Toastmaster and former Presidents Distinguished Division Governor in Toastmasters and winner of Division Governor of the Year award, has been in IT since 1999, first as a developer then 7 years ago she became a Solutions Architect at Verizon. Bett also cohosts the Software Architecture Concepts Podcast. Now, she is driving Customer Experience Architecture at Verizon to improve the processes and the customer experience and the manager of the IT Verizon Leadership Development Program. Her books are available on Amazon.com and Audible.com. Bett also freelances as a "Book Project Manager" to help "authors-in-the-making" make their dreams of being a published author a reality.

Bett has several more books coming out soon. Keep up on the latest of her events, books, articles, speaking engagements.

Follow her on Twitter @betterworkINC.

Follow her blog at www.betterworkinc.com

Sign up for her newsletter at http://eepurl.com/f_ETX

Blog Link   Newsletter Link

www.ingramcontent.com/pod-product-compliance
Lightning Source LLC
Chambersburg PA
CBHW070342290526
45791CB00003B/1445